THE CITY

LIFE IN ANCIENT EGYPT

THE CITY

BY

KATHRYN HINDS

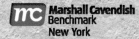
mc Marshall Cavendish
Benchmark
New York

To Owen

The author and publisher wish to specially thank J. Brett McClain of the Oriental Institute of the University of Chicago for his invaluable help in reviewing the manuscript.

MARSHALL CAVENDISH BENCHMARK 99 WHITE PLAINS ROAD TARRYTOWN, NEW YORK 10591-9001
www.marshallcavendish.us

LIBRARY OF CONGRESS CATALOGING-IN-PUBLICATION DATA: Hinds, Kathryn, 1962- The city : by Kathryn Hinds. p. cm. — (Life in ancient Egypt) Summary: "Describes daily life in the cities of ancient Egypt during the New Kingdom period, from about 1550 BCE to about 1070 BCE, including the roles of women and men and what it was like to be a child in that era"—Provided by publisher. Includes bibliographical references and index. ISBN-13: 978-0-7614-2184-9   ISBN-10: 0-7614-2184-X 1. Egypt—Social life and customs—To 332 BC—Juvenile literature.   2. Cities and towns, Ancient—Egypt—Juvenile literature. I. Title. II. Series. DT61.H479 2006   932'.009732—dc22   2005033681

EDITOR: Joyce Stanton   EDITORIAL DIRECTOR: Michelle Bisson
ART DIRECTOR: Anahid Hamparian   SERIES DESIGNER: Michael Nelson

Images provided by Rose Corbett Gordon, Art Editor, Mystic CT, from the following sources: Cover: Massimo Listri/Corbis back cover: Valley of the Nobles, Thebes, Egypt/Giraudon/ The Bridgeman Art Library, page i: Louvre, Paris/Bridgeman Art Library; pages iii, 32, 53: Gianni Dagli Orti/Corbis; pages vi, 38: The Art Archive/Dagli Orti; pages viii, 6, 61: The Granger Collection, NY; page 2: Photri/Topham/The Image Works; page 3: The Art Archive/Château de Thoiry/Dagli Orti; page 7: Valley of the Nobles, Thebes, Egypt/Giraudon/The Bridgeman Art Library; page 9: The Art Archive/Museo Naval Madrid/Dagli Orti; pages 10, 11, 12, 19: HIP/ Art Resource, NY; pages 15, 18, 29, 40, 46, 58: Erich Lessing/Art Resource, NY; pages 10, 11, 12, 19: HIP/Art Resource, NY; page 16: C.Walker/Topham/The Image Works; page 17: The Art Archive/Bibliothèque des Arts Décoratifs Paris/Dagli Orti; pages 20, 25, 28, 51: The Art Archive/Egyptian Museum Cairo/Dagli Orti; page 22: Werner Forman/Art Resource, NY; page 24: Bequest of Mrs. Carl L. Selden, Brooklyn Museum of Art/ Bridgeman Art Library; pages 27, 48: The Art Archive/Musée du Louvre/Dagli Orti; pages 30, 42: Ashmolean Museum, University of Oxford/Bridgeman Art Library; page 34: The Art Archive/Museum voor Shone Kunsten Ghent/Dagli Orti; pages 36, 56: The Art Archive/Archaeological Museum Bologna/Dagli Orti; page 37: Werner Forman Archive/Egyptian Museum Cairo/The Image Works; page 43: Bojan Brecelj/Corbis; page 45: Oriental Museum/Durham University/Bridgeman Art Library; page 52: Charles & Josette Lenars/Corbis; page 54: British Museum/ Bridgeman Art Library.

Printed in China
135642

front cover: A nineteenth-century artist's imaginative reconstruction of the city of Thebes
half-title page: A cat mummy from the city of Bubastis in the Nile Delta
title page: Women share fruit and sniff lotus flowers at a banquet.
page vi: A boat's crew uses both sails and oars to travel on the Nile River.
back cover: A laborer makes careful measurements at a construction site.

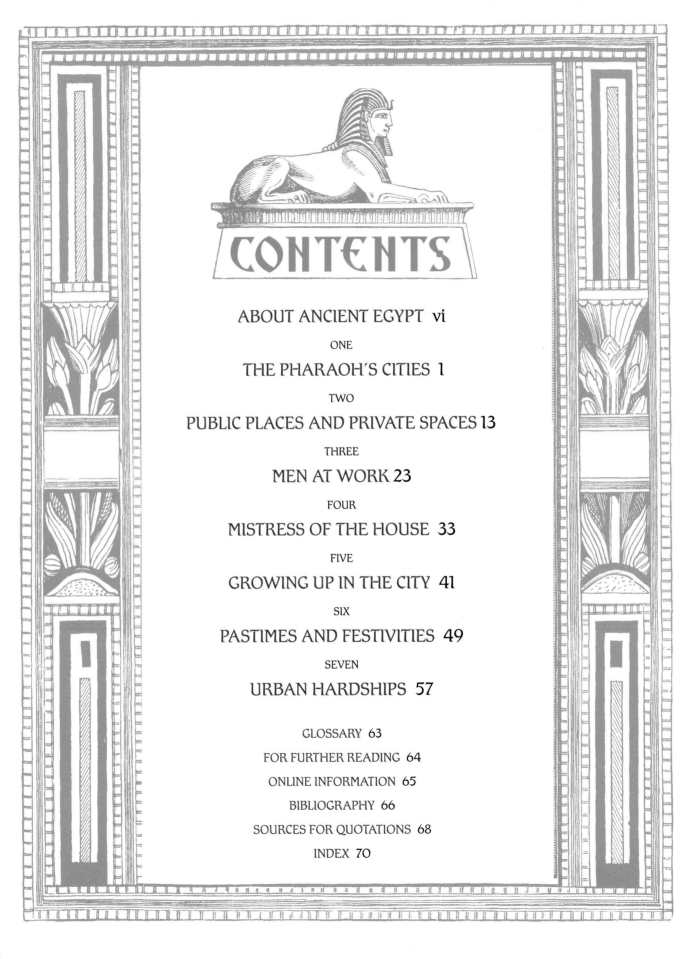

CONTENTS

ABOUT ANCIENT EGYPT

When we think about ancient Egypt, magnificent images immediately come to mind: the pyramids, the Sphinx, the golden funeral mask of "King Tut," colossal statues of mighty kings. Our imaginations are full of mummies and tombs, hieroglyphic symbols and animal-headed goddesses and gods. Most of us, however, don't often give much thought to the people of ancient Egypt and how they lived their everyday lives. Where would we even start?

Ancient Egyptian history is vast—about three thousand years long, in fact, from the first known pharaoh (Aha, also called Menes) to the last independent ruler (Cleopatra VII). During this span of time, Egyptian society and culture naturally underwent many changes. So to make it easier to get to know the people of ancient Egypt, this series of books focuses on a smaller chunk of history, the period known as the New Kingdom, from about 1550 to about 1070 BCE. This was the era of ancient Egypt's greatest power and the time of some of its most famous pharaohs, or rulers: Hatshepsut, Thutmose III, Amenhotep III, Akhenaten, Tutankhamen, Ramses II.

During the New Kingdom, Egypt was the dominant force in the Mediterranean world—a true superpower. The pharaohs controlled territory from Syria to what is now Sudan, and their influence stretched to Asia Minor and Mesopotamia. Yet no matter how wide their connections, the Egyptians maintained a unique culture with its own writing, artistic style, religion, type of government, and social organization. And always at the center of life was the Nile River, which made Egypt a long, narrow oasis of greenery in the midst of the desert.

In this book you will meet the people of ancient Egypt's cities: government officials, scribes, craftspeople, housewives, children. You will visit homes, markets, temples, and fortresses. You will learn how Egyptian city dwellers relaxed, and you will also see some of the hardships they suffered. So step back into history, to a time even before the splendors of ancient Greece and Rome. Welcome to life in ancient Egypt!

A variety of systems of dating have been used by different cultures throughout history. Many historians now prefer to use BCE (Before Common Era) and CE (Common Era) instead of BC (Before Christ) and AD (Anno Domini), out of respect for the diversity of the world's peoples.

ONE

THE PHARAOH'S CITIES

uring the New Kingdom, Egypt boasted two great capital cities that served as centers of government, religion, and the arts: Memphis in the north, and Thebes in the south. For a brief period, during the reign of Akhenaten (1352–1336 BCE), the brand-new city of Amarna in middle Egypt became the country's capital. Later, Ramses II (1279–1213 BCE) built the royal city of Pi-Ramses, in the Nile Delta, and moved the center of government there. Egypt also possessed a number of smaller cities. The country was divided into forty-two regions or provinces, and each had its own capital. Other cities and towns grew up around religious sites or fortresses. Large or small, all Egyptian cities—like everything else in Egypt—were regarded as belonging to the pharaoh.

The royal presence was felt everywhere. A pharaoh rarely spent all his time in the capital, where his main palace was. He might often be out of the country leading his troops in battle. At home in

Opposite:
Carpenters like these were among the many craftspeople whose work made ancient Egyptian cities thrive.

1

Egypt, he would cruise up and down the Nile to visit the different parts of his realm. He therefore had residences in many cities—smaller palaces that were known as Landing Places of the King. When the ruler was not present in a city in person, he could rely on various government administrators to act on his behalf. At the same time, public buildings were adorned with statues and reliefs depicting the pharaoh and his mighty ancestors. Egyptian city dwellers always knew that they and their nation were watched over by the greatest of mortals, the favored child of the gods.

This satellite photo clearly shows the fertile green land watered by the Nile River in the midst of the desert.

MEMPHIS

Throughout ancient Egyptian history, Memphis was well populated and important, and famous throughout the Mediterranean world. At different times it bore different names: Ineb-hedj, "White Walls," probably referred to the walls of the royal palace. Ankh-tawy, "That Which Binds the Two Lands," expressed the city's location at the base of the delta, the place where Lower (northern) and Upper (southern) Egypt met. Another name, Men-nefer, meant "Established and Beautiful"; it was eventually turned into "Memphis" by the Greeks.

Men-nefer was originally just the name of the cemetery where Old Kingdom pharaoh Pepi I was buried. Indeed, part of Memphis's claim to fame has always been the extensive necropolis, or burial ground, outside the city. The most

renowned tombs in the area were and are the pyramids—not only the Great Pyramid of Khufu and its companions at Giza, but also the Step Pyramid at Saqqara, the Bent Pyramid at Dahshur, and more than thirty others. Several of the pyramids were major pilgrimage sites or tourist attractions during the New Kingdom.

The pyramids, along with numerous other tombs, were built in the desert so, thanks to the dry conditions there, have survived better than most of riverside Memphis. Not including the necropolis, the city probably covered about three square miles, but much of the area has been built over or flooded. In addition, during the Middle Ages the remains of ancient buildings were dismantled and the stone was taken to construct the city of Cairo, a few miles to the northeast. Memphis was one of Egypt's earliest and longest-lasting capitals. Today Cairo is the capital of the modern nation.

The pyramids of Giza as they appeared in the early 1800s. Notice how similar the boat in the foreground is to that shown on page vi.

THEBES AND AVARIS

Thebes is the name that the Greeks gave to the city known to the ancient Egyptians as Waset. Thebes also had an often-used nickname, Niwt, meaning simply "The City." A New Kingdom poem

HITTITE EMPIRE

ASIA MINOR
(ANATOLIA)

GREECE

MITANNI

MESOPOTAMIA

TIGRIS RIVER

SYRIA

LEBANON

EUPHRATES RIVER

MEDITERRANEAN SEA

Megiddo ⊙

JORDAN RIVER

Babylon ⊙

NILE DELTA

LOWER
EGYPT

LIBYA

Avaris ⊙
Pi-Ramses ⊙
Bubastis ⊙
Giza ⊙⊙
Saqqara ⊙⊙ Memphis
Dahshur ⊙

NILE RIVER

SINAI

EGYPT
AND ITS NEIGHBORS
DURING THE
NEW KINGDOM

SAHARA

EGYPT

Amarna ⊙

UPPER EGYPT

N
W ✦ E
S

Valley of the Kings ⊙ ⊙ Thebes
Deir el-Medina ⊙

RED SEA

NUBIA

Abu Simbel ⊙
Buhen ⊙

MILES

0   100   200

EGYPTIAN–RULED
TERRITORY
IN THE 1400s BCE

praised Thebes as "the pattern for every city. Both water and earth were within her from the beginning of time. . . . So mankind came into being within her, with the purpose of founding every city in her proper name. For all are called 'City' after the example of Thebes."

Throughout the Middle Kingdom, Thebes had been a regional power center in southern Egypt. It came to national importance during a time when Egypt was divided and the Theban ruling family fought to take northern Egypt from the Hyksos. For nearly a hundred years, the north had been ruled by the Hyksos, or "Foreign Princes," originally from southwestern Asia. Avaris, the Hyksos capital city, was naturally a focus of this war. As King Kamose of Thebes recorded in an inscription, "I did not leave a scrap of Avaris without being empty . . . I laid waste their towns and burned their places, they being made into red ruins for eternity on account of the damage which they did within this Egypt, for they had made themselves serve the Asiatic and had forsaken Egypt their mistress." It was Kamose's brother Ahmose who defeated the Hyksos once and for all, becoming king of a reunited Egypt; this was the beginning of the New Kingdom and of the Eighteenth Dynasty of pharaohs.

Avaris was probably not destroyed as thoroughly as Kamose claimed, for Ahmose took up residence there. Because of its location in the eastern delta, it was an excellent base for his military actions against the Hyksos' allies in the area that is, roughly, modern Israel. But Ahmose's son, Amenhotep I (1525–1504 BCE), seems to have favored the family's hometown. Amenhotep began an enthusiastic program of beautifying and developing Thebes and the surrounding area. His successors continued to build up Thebes, which they showered with the riches they gained from their wars and diplomatic arrangements with neighboring countries. Even at a later period, the ancient Greek poet Homer was moved to comment on "all the wealth that goes into Thebes of Egypt, where treasures in greatest store are laid up in men's houses. Thebes, which is the city of an hundred gates and from each issue forth to do battle two hundred doughty warriors with horses and chariots."

Ahmose and Amenhotep added another sort of glory to Thebes by having their tombs dug near the city (most previous kings had been buried in the region around Memphis). The exact location of these tombs is still not known, but Egyptologists are certain of the final resting place of the next ruler, Thutmose I. He was buried in the desert cliffs across the Nile from Thebes, in the famous royal cemetery called the Valley of the Kings. Nearly all the New Kingdom pharaohs were eventually buried there.

The digging, decorating, and supplying of the royal tombs provided constant employment for a good number of people. These necropolis workers lived in a village, said to have been founded by Amenhotep I, in the desert near the Valley of the Kings. Known now as Deir el-Medina, this settlement was occupied for hundreds of years. Because of its location far from the river and farmland, its ruins

The ruins of Deir el-Medina, the walled town that was home to some of the New Kingdom's most skilled and privileged workers

were well preserved, and it has provided archaeologists with a great deal of precious information about everyday life in ancient Egypt.

AMARNA

Amarna is the modern name usually given to ancient Akhetaten, which means "Horizon of the Aten." The Aten was the visible disk of the sun and the favorite deity of the pharaoh Akhenaten. After four years on the throne, he decided to leave Thebes and found a new capital, dedicated to the Aten, on a site where no settlement or temple had ever stood before. An inscription records the pharaoh's words about the founding of his city: "Behold Akhetaten which the Aten desires me to make unto him as a monument in his name for ever."

Amarna was situated on the east bank of the Nile almost exactly midway between Memphis and Thebes. The pharaoh's workers built it with amazing speed: construction started in the fifth year of Akhenaten's reign, and the city was occupied and in full use by the ninth year. Archaeologists have discovered that, in fact, some of the work was rather shoddy—many imperfections in the walls of buildings were disguised by thick layers of plaster. Palaces, temples, and the main road were carefully planned, but other city streets and buildings arranged themselves without any particular order. On the other hand, the workmen's village east of the city was precisely laid out, with the houses in straight rows along five streets. The residents

Workers make mud bricks and build a wall.

of this village may have been "imported" from Deir el-Medina. Their job was to construct and supply the tombs in the cemetery that Akhenaten ordered built in the cliffs that marked the eastern boundary of his city.

Amarna was abandoned after Akhenaten died. When the throne passed to Tutankhamen, he chose Memphis as his main base. Most of Amarna's residents followed the king north, or returned to their former homes in Thebes and the surrounding area. Because Amarna was in a somewhat isolated location and was occupied for only a short time, it is the best preserved of all Egyptian cities. It is far enough from the river to avoid flooding, and no one has ever built on top of it. Archaeologists have been able to study extensive remains, contributing much of what we know about urban life in ancient Egypt.

PI-RAMSES

Ramses II, the greatest king of the Nineteenth Dynasty, belonged to a family that came from the region of Avaris. The old Hyksos capital was still a thriving center of commerce, according to writings of this period. When Ramses decided he needed a new capital, he built it near Avaris, which probably continued to act as his city's port.

The full name of Ramses' capital was Pi-Ramses Aa-nakhtu, "The Domain of Ramses Great-of-Victories." A writer of the time commented, "His Majesty has built himself a Residence whose name is 'Great-of-Victories.' It lies between Syria and Egypt, full of food and provisions. The Sun arises in its horizon, and [even] sets within it. Everyone has left his own town and settles in its neighborhood." There might not have been room for "everyone" to settle in Pi-Ramses, but it clearly was a large and magnificent city, covering several square miles. It was said to be "beauteous of balconies, dazzling with halls of lapis and turquoise. [The young men of the city]

are in festival dress daily, oil on their heads, hair freshly set. They stand by their doors, hands bowed down with foliage and greenery."

Ramses' great city was built beside a branch of the Nile that eventually dried up. The city, too, declined, and over time the urban landscape was replaced with marshes and farmland. For centuries the location of Pi-Ramses was lost. Archaeologists, however, have finally rediscovered the pharaoh's great capital. Their excavations so far show that about half the city seems to have been taken up by a military compound, with drill fields, stables for chariots and horses, and a variety of workshops. Another discovery was a large facility for smelting and casting metal; it was probably used mainly for producing the army's bronze weapons. Ramses spent part of his reign fighting the Hittites of Asia Minor, but eventually made peace with them, sealing the treaty by marrying a Hittite princess. Hittite arrowheads, lance points, bronze scales from armor, and molds for making metal shield fittings have been found at Pi-Ramses, showing that the peace gave Ramses access to advanced Hittite military technology. It may be that there was even a group of Hittite metalworkers living in the city. Pi-Ramses, with its easy access to the Mediterranean Sea and to the land routes to Asia, must have been a center of international trade and politics—a fitting capital for the richest, most powerful nation of the time.

Ancient Egyptian ships sail into the Mediterranean Sea, as imagined by a nineteenth-century artist.

A Note on Dates, Dynasties, and Names

The dates of the pharaohs' reigns and the spelling of their names used in this book generally follow *The Oxford History of Ancient Egypt,* edited by Ian Shaw. However, if you continue to study ancient Egypt, you will see other dates and other spellings. Here's why:

The ancient Egyptians did not calculate dates by numbering the years from a single fixed starting point as we do. Instead, they numbered the years from the beginning of each pharaoh's reign. For example, they would record events as taking place in the second year of the reign of Tutankhamen or the tenth year of the reign of Horemheb. It is often difficult to convert Egyptian dates to our dating system, so various sources give differing dates for the events of ancient Egyptian history. For this reason, all dates in this book must be considered approximate.

Scholars have traditionally divided the three thousand years of ancient Egyptian history into the following eras: the Early Dynastic Period, the Old Kingdom, the First Intermediate Period, the Middle Kingdom, the Second Intermediate Period, the New Kingdom, the Third Intermediate Period, the Late Period, and the Greco-Roman Period.

The New Kingdom was comprised of three dynasties: the Eighteenth (1550–1295 BCE), Nineteenth (1295–1186 BCE), and Twentieth (1186–1069 BCE). The Eighteenth Dynasty occupies roughly the middle of ancient Egypt's history as an independent nation.

As for names, the ancient Egyptian language poses a unique set of problems. Scholars have been able to read Egyptian hieroglyphs—the famous pictures signs of ancient

Above: Columns of hieroglyphs in a papyrus book that was buried with a government official

Egypt—since 1822. But most hieroglyphs did not stand for individual letters and their sounds, as in our alphabet. A few hieroglyphs represented single consonants, but most of them stood for groups of consonants or for entire words or concepts. Vowels were rarely indicated. These facts have made it a challenge for Egyptologists to decide on the best way to use our alphabet to spell ancient Egyptian names and words. Different spellings have been preferred at different times and places, and even today there is no agreement among scholars on exact spellings.

From the same book, scenes of funeral offerings and the beautiful fields of the afterlife

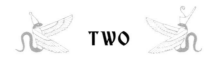

TWO

PUBLIC PLACES AND PRIVATE SPACES

gypt's population during the New Kingdom was approximately 3 million. Scholars estimate that only about 5 percent—150,000 people—lived in towns or cities. Yet the city was a place where people of all types came together: government officials, priests, soldiers, merchants, craftspeople, housewives, entertainers, donkey drivers, and laborers. Cities were not only socially but also ethnically diverse, home or stopping places for traders, entertainers, artisans, and even mercenaries from many parts of the eastern Mediterranean. All these types of people mixed freely in Egypt's crowded cities.

In Amarna the wealthy occupied spacious villas. The small houses of poorer people clustered around the villas, in the spaces between them. It seems that other cities may have followed a similar pattern—or lack of pattern—in frequently mingling rich and poor in the same neighborhood. There do seem to be a few exam-

Opposite:
A New Kingdom official's home, with roof vents to capture the cooling northern breezes and a garden with palm and sycamore trees to provide shade

ples of slum areas, however, such as one near the docks in Amarna's northern suburb.

Neighborhoods around the wharves were often home to merchants, too, who liked having easy access to the ships that carried goods up and down the Nile. Similarly, priests tended to have their houses near the temples they served. Sometimes people in the same craft or trade—brewers, sandal makers, or scribes, for instance—would live next to each other. In western Thebes Egyptologists found that one group that clustered together was made up of people who worked the land. Many of them lived in the very southwest of the city, probably because the fields they tended were close by.

The division between city and country was not always as firm as it is today. In fact, some Egyptians felt that including rural areas within city limits reflected a kind of divine perfection. Akhenaten, for example, marked out an area roughly ten by eight miles for Amarna. Even with its suburbs, however, the actual city did not fill all this area. Akhenaten planned it that way, both so that there would be room for the settlement to grow and so that it could contain "mountains, deserts, meadows, water, villages, embankments, men, beasts, groves and all things which the Aten shall bring into existence."

CENTERS OF CEREMONY

Cities were both symbols and centers of the pharaoh's power, so it is no surprise that royal residences and government offices formed part of the urban landscape. But the buildings that kings most relied on to demonstrate their magnificence were the temples.

Often built on a colossal scale, temples were meant to last through the ages—as many, in fact, have done. Their stone walls and gateways were carved with scenes of kings in action, accompanied by hieroglyphic texts, as well as with images of goddesses and gods.

FORTRESS TOWNS

In most of Egypt, the vast desert was all the protection needed from raids or invasion attempts. In the north, however, the country was less secure, for Libyans might attack from the west, while peoples from what is now the land of Israel could threaten from the east. The south, too, was vulnerable, with its shifting border between Egypt and Nubia. The pharaohs protected these areas with fortified towns that housed garrisons of soldiers, who patrolled the borders and could stand as the first line of defense in case of trouble.

The fortress towns of Nubia guarded not only Egypt's frontier and Nubian conquests, but also the trade route between Egypt and sub-Saharan Africa. An impressive example was the fortress at Buhen, about 150 miles from the ancient Egyptian border. On the west bank of the Nile, it was founded during the Old Kingdom, strengthened during the Middle Kingdom, and occupied by more and more civilians during the New Kingdom. It was surrounded by a ditch and a high mud-brick wall, thirteen feet thick in places. The main

Soldiers on parade carry fans and palm branches as well as axes and throwing sticks.

entrance was guarded by a tower and drawbridge. Within the wall was a neat grid of streets with several blocks of housing for the soldiers and, at least for officers, their families. No doubt craftsmen who made armor, weapons, and other things needed by the garrison also lived in this area. One whole block was taken up by the commander's residence; half of another block was occupied by a temple. There would also have been facilities such as stables and storehouses.

Some fortresses in Nubia also played nonmilitary roles: one seems to have been a storage depot for grain; another had facilities for processing gold. Such nonmilitary functions gradually increased. During the New Kingdom, Egypt had such a secure hold on Nubia that people felt safe settling outside the fortresses, building unprotected homes, temples, and businesses.

An artist's reconstruction of the great columned hall in the temple of Karnak

During the first half of the Eighteenth Dynasty, Thebes grew to become an impressive religious center, with many temples. Most important was the temple complex of Karnak, dedicated to Amen, who was the patron god of Thebes and of the early New Kingdom pharaohs. King after king added gateways, obelisks, pillared halls, courtyards, and chapels to Karnak, each ruler trying to outdo his predecessor. One of the greatest honors a nonroyal Egyptian could receive was to be allowed to have a statue of himself within the temple complex; only very favored and high-ranking government officials achieved this.

Much of the magnificence of an ancient Egyptian temple was seen by a limited number of people—most of the building was open only to priests and other temple employees. The innermost part of a temple was reserved for the pharaoh and for the highest-ranking priests to make offerings to the deity to whom the temple was dedicated. On the other hand, the outer courtyards were open to everyone, especially on holidays, when people of all ranks gathered to watch special ceremonies and processions.*

HOME SWEET HOME

The houses of the gods were made of stone, but human dwellings were built with mud bricks, molded in wooden frames and baked hard under the hot Egyptian sun. Even royal palaces were constructed of this simple material, which was easy to obtain and easy to make. But although building materials were the same for the

*To read more about temples and their activities, see the *Religion* volume of this series.

powerful and the humble, it was easy to tell the houses of the rich from those of the poor.

In Amarna high officials lived in villas that were often set within a large walled compound or courtyard. The whole complex could include a well, a chapel, storage areas, servants' quarters, stables, kitchens, and gardens with flowers, fishponds, and date trees. The house itself typically had twenty to twenty-eight rooms. The largest was generally one of the front rooms, with a high ceiling supported by painted wooden pillars. The front was the most public part of the villa, used for receiving guests and holding banquets and parties. The further into the house a room was, the more private it was—so the family's bedrooms were likely at the back, farthest from the street.

This is what a wealthy Egyptian's villa may have looked like.

In Thebes and Memphis, cities that were far older and more built-up than Amarna, the wealthy were a bit more crowded than this. There was no room for compounds with gardens and courtyards and sprawling one-story houses in the Amarna style. Still, the two- or three-story homes of the well-to-do were very spacious compared to those of the average Egyptian.

Many examples of workers' houses have been found at Amarna. Almost all had a three-part structure: the front and center sections were each an entire room, and the back was divided into two rooms.

There were also stairs at the backs of many houses, but archaeologists cannot be sure whether these led to a second story or just to the roof. Roofs were flat, providing an extra place where the family could work or relax. People often slept on their roofs, too, lying on straw mats to enjoy the fresh air on summer nights.

The homes of the wealthy were distinguished not only by their size, but also by their comforts and conveniences. Along with a private well, an upper-class Egyptian's house frequently included a bathroom. Lined with sheets of limestone, and with a drain in the stone floor, this was basically an early form of shower stall: the bather stood here while servants poured jars of water over him or her. A nearby room sometimes provided for other bathroom needs with one or two seats raised up on bricks, with bowls of sand beneath. A portable version of this arrangement was the closestool—

Potters put the finishing touches on a large storage jar by polishing it with stones.

a stool that had an opening in the top and enclosed a chamber pot. The average city dweller, however, had no bathroom facilities of any kind, except for a box of sand or a closes-tool. To get water, most people had to go to a well that they shared with their neighbors.

Well-off Egyptians furnished their homes with elegant wooden chairs, tables (generally only large enough for two people to sit at), and storage chests. They also stored things in baskets and pottery jars. Men and women both had makeup cases of wood or alabaster and mirrors made of polished metal—makeup was not just for adornment, but also helped protect against the sun. Dishes, cups, and other vessels might be made of metal or of alabaster or other kinds of stone. The Eighteenth Dynasty also saw the beginning of Egyptian glassworking, providing the well-to-do with jars, bottles, and vases made of multicolored glass in a distinctive wavy pattern. Modern Egyptian craftspeople still make this kind of glass, keeping alive techniques and designs that are more than three thousand years old. In fact, many of the arts and crafts of today's Egypt show ancient influences.

Affluent people owned wooden-framed beds with "mattresses" of folded linen pads over "springs" of woven leather strips. Since an Egyptian bed slanted downward, it always needed a footboard to keep the sleeper from sliding out of bed. There was no pillow, only a shoulder-height, curved headrest, usually made of wood. The average person, however, might not be able to afford this kind of

The colorful wave patterns seen on this ancient glass bottle in the shape of a fish are typical of modern hand-crafted Egyptian glassware, too.

A painted plaster floor from a palace in Amarna. New Kingdom Egyptians were fond of scenes from nature such as this.

bed. Instead, a typical worker's home featured a built-in brick platform that served as a couch by day and a bed by night. Some nonwealthy people owned headrests, too. But in many cases, the poor probably slept on straw mats on the floor.

It seems that Egyptians of all classes enjoyed color and decoration in their homes. Many of the workers' houses in Deir el-Medina were whitewashed on the outside, their front doors painted red. The inside walls might also be whitewashed, sometimes with the colorful addition of murals. Some householders hung their walls with multicolored mats made of woven reeds. Designs in yellow and blue paint often adorned columns and framed windows and doors. The villas of the wealthy were even more artistically decorated, with finely painted floors and ceilings as well as walls. The most beautiful of the surviving murals show scenes from nature; simpler colored borders or geometric designs have also been found.

Rich or poor, all Egyptians shared certain living conditions. Everyone had to cope with Egypt's intense heat, so houses were well insulated with walls that might be twenty inches thick. Many dwellings had roof vents designed to catch "the sweet breath of the north wind." Windows were small and placed up high, so little sunlight came in. While this helped keep the houses relatively cool, it also made them quite dark. The only artificial light available was provided by oil lamps. On cold winter nights, extra heat might be supplied by braziers—which only warmed you if you were sitting right next to one.

THREE

MEN AT WORK

Among the many precious documents studied by Egyptologists, there is one from the late twelfth century BCE that gives us a clear, though fleeting, glimpse of an urban community. This sheet of papyrus contains a register from a section of western Thebes, and it lists 182 householders, giving not only the men's names but their occupations. Other town registers that have been found have focused on elite citizens: administrators, scribes, priests, and soldiers. But the document from western Thebes also includes men in humbler trades, including an overseer, a goldsmith, coppersmiths, sandal makers, brewers, incense makers, gardeners, stablemen, fishermen, and herdsmen. Egyptian society had a place for everyone, from the lowliest laborer to the highest official, and each had his role to play in the proper order of things.

Opposite:
A carpenter, perched in a building's scaffolding, hews at a piece of wood with his bronze adze.

23

A mayor or other high official holds his staff of office, a symbol of his authority.

THE MEN IN CHARGE

As powerful as the pharaoh was, he was only one man (or, on a few occasions, woman), and he could not personally control everything in Egypt. He had his representatives throughout the country, men who could report back to him and act on his behalf. Every city therefore was governed by a mayor. Mayors were chosen and overseen by the king's viziers, the highest government officials next to the king himself. There were two viziers: one with authority over the north and the other over the south. Generally the viziers were based in Memphis and Thebes.

A city's mayor had the responsibility for putting royal plans and commands into action in his locality. Moreover, he was responsible for seeing that taxes were properly collected and sent to the royal treasuries and storehouses. Since the Egyptians of this time did not use coins or other standard types of money, this task could be fairly complicated. Farmers' taxes were paid with grain, livestock, or produce of various kinds; craftspeople paid by turning over some of the goods they made. The mayor's staff figured out just how much every citizen owed, but sometimes the mayor himself had to go and personally collect payments. For example, Sennefer, mayor of Thebes, sent this letter to a farmer who was slow in paying up:

KEEPING THE PEACE

Soldiers were stationed in Egypt's capitals, and probably in many other cities as well. Their duties included patrolling the city limits, as shown by the still-visible track worn by the pacing of soldiers on Amarna's eastern boundary. Soldiers or police officers also protected palaces, temples, mines, waterways, and tombs. They patrolled the deserts, too, on the watch for criminals, escaped prisoners, foreign spies, and troublemaking nomads.

During the New Kingdom, Egypt had a special police force known as the Medjay, descendants of Nubian mercenaries. Their duties included maintaining security in the villages of tomb workers, guarding royal tombs during construction, inspecting tombs for signs of break-in or theft; chasing down, questioning, and punishing thieves; and carrying official messages. Sometimes they also acted as a bodyguard or honor guard for the king, but they might also help out the tomb workers with such tasks as moving stone blocks.

The Medjay chief who kept the peace in Amarna was a powerful and favored man named Mahu. He was given the title General of the Army of the Lord of the Two Lands and had the assistance of several army commanders, along with battalions of both foot soldiers and cavalry. Mahu was an active man, enthusiastic about his job. An inscription from his tomb tells how he was awakened early one morning by the news that foreign criminals were in the city. Mahu leaped out of bed and into his chariot in pursuit of the foreigners. With the help of six of his Medjay, armed with short staffs and forked sticks, he captured the criminals and personally took them to the vizier for judgment. For this and other services, the king rewarded Mahu with a gold collar, Egypt's highest honor.

Above: Officials and military officers who served the pharaoh especially well were rewarded with heavy collars called the Gold of Praise.

This letter is sent to you to inform you that I shall reach you . . . in three days. Don't let me catch you out in your position. Don't let it be lacking in very good order. And gather for me many plants, lotus blooms, flowers . . . ready to be used as offerings. And cut 5,000 pieces of wood. . . . Then the boat which will bring me will take them away. For you have cut no wood this year. . . . And instruct the herdsmen to get milk ready anew in jars in advance of my coming. Look out! You should not be lazy; for I am well aware that you are lackadaisical, and like eating in bed.

Another important government institution in an Egyptian city was the *kenbet,* or council. Thebes and Memphis each had a great *kenbet,* headed by the vizier, and composed of high-ranking officials, priests, and military men. These great councils functioned largely as courts of law for important civil cases. The regional *kenbets* of other cities, made up of leading citizens, judged smaller matters, such as local property disputes. They also conducted trials for a variety of common crimes. The most serious crimes, however, were judged by the vizier himself.

MASTERS OF THE WRITTEN WORD

The most prestigious jobs in Egypt were always held by men who had been educated as scribes, experts in reading and writing. A man with scribal training could rise very high indeed—as books written by scribes never tired of pointing out. The craft of a scribe "is better than all crafts; it promotes people. He who is accomplished in it is found suitable to be an official," says one source. Moreover, "there is no profession free of a boss, except for that of the scribe—*he* is the boss."

The rewards of a scribal career were both material and spiritual: "A country-house is built (for you) in your city, and you possess a powerful position by the gift of the king to you." And after death, a scribe's writings would cause his name to live on, guaranteeing him eternal life:

> A man is perished, his corpse is dust, all his contemporaries have gone to dust; but it is writing which causes him to be remembered in the mouth of him who utters [the prayers for the dead]. More beneficial is writing than the house of a builder, or tombs in the West. It is better than an established [mansion], or a stela in the temple.

A scribe dips his stylus, or reed brush, into the ink on his wooden palette. He keeps a spare stylus tucked behind his ear.

Some scribes did indeed fulfill the promise of high rank and royal favor. Their mastery of writing allowed them to hold influential positions in the government, military, and priesthood. For others, their literacy qualified them to become doctors or architects or what we would think of as lawyers. Most scribes, however, probably functioned mainly as what we would call secretaries and accountants.

Temples and government offices employed large numbers of scribes to keep records and copy out documents. A good number of scribes were members of wealthy households, where they acted as private secretaries, kept the family's accounts, and perhaps supervised other household employees. People of more modest means hired scribes whenever they needed letters written—or, for that matter, read. Many scribes also made at least part of their living by teaching reading and writing to future scribes. And they never hesitated to remind their students that even the humblest scribe had at least one advantage over other workers: "There is no tax levied on him who works in writing."

SUCCESS IN THE CRAFTS

A potter squats on the ground as he shapes a pot from wet clay.

Scribal teachers tried many ways to motivate their pupils to work hard, including having them copy out texts that described the difficulties and annoyances of other occupations. *The Satire on the Trades,* originally composed during the Middle Kingdom, was one of these. Although its descriptions are exaggerated, it does give us vivid pictures of various crafts and trades. We read that "any carpenter who takes up the adze becomes more tired than the worker on the land. His field is the wood, and his hoe is the adze. There is no limit to his work; he labours beyond what his arms can do." The coppersmith "at his work at the mouth of his furnace" has fingers like crocodile skin and "stinks more than fish eggs." Worse still is the lot of potters:

> The potter is under the soil, although he stands
>   among the living.
> He grubs in the mud more than a pig in order
>   to bake his pots.
> His clothes are stiff with clay, his loincloth in rags.
> Breath enters his nose direct from the furnace.
> He tramples [the clay] with his feet, and is
>   himself crushed by it.

Even jewelers, perhaps the most elite among all craftsmen, are portrayed with an emphasis on the hardships of their trade:

> The jeweller is boring carefully into every type of
>   hard stone.
> He completes the inlay of an eye; his arms are exhausted
>   and he is weary.
> He sits at sunset, with his knees and his back cramped. . . .

No doubt these artisans did work extremely hard and often suffered from exhaustion, sore backs, cramped hands, and the like. But many, while not wealthy, were well-off and enjoyed a comfortable standard of living. The craftsmen who worked on the royal tombs were given their houses and all the rations they needed by the state. They put in four hours of work in the morning then, after lunch and a nap, four more hours in the afternoon. After they had worked eight days in a row, they received two days off. The artisans employed by temples and palaces probably enjoyed similar conditions. Even craftsmen who worked out of their own homes, producing goods for use by their fellow city dwellers, were certainly better off than unskilled workers such as porters and donkey drivers.

The artisans of the New Kingdom made do with tools of

Brick making was a tiresome job, but an essential one.

Musicians, like this man from western Asia, were among the Egyptian city dwellers who made their living in the arts.

bronze, copper, stone, or wood, with few mechanical aids. What they accomplished in stone, wood, paint, metal, ivory, glass, and gems was truly astonishing. In spite of the mockery of *The Satire on the Trades,* these craftsmen knew their own worth, and so did others. Pharaoh Ramses II (1279–1213 BCE) handpicked some of the sculptors who worked on his temples and did not hesitate to praise them: "You chosen workmen, valiant men of proven skill, craftsmen in valuable stone, experienced in granite, familiar with quartzite, good fellows tireless and vigilant at work all day. I am your constant provider. I know your labors to be eager. . . ."

Indeed, we can believe that many craftsmen took great pride and satisfaction in their work. This is certainly the feeling expressed by the Middle Kingdom sculptor Iritsen:

I am a craftsman successful in his craft, one who comes out on top through that which he knows. . . . I

know the movement of a figure, the stride of a woman
. . . the cringing of the solitary captive, how one eye
looks at another, how to make frightened the face of
the outlaw, the pose of the arm of him who harpoons
the hippopotamus, the pace of the runner.

It is thanks to Iritsen and people like him that we have such a
wealth of images of life in ancient Egypt, not to mention some of
the world's greatest art.

FOUR

MISTRESS OF THE HOUSE

Egyptian women were better off than women in much of the ancient world. In fact, they had legal rights that women in Europe and the Americas began to win only in the late nineteenth century. They could, for example, own property, testify in court, make contracts, and get divorced. At the same time, women's roles were distinctly different from men's. Generally speaking, women worked in the home, men outside of it. Both kinds of work received respect, however, because this division of labor was seen as a natural balance, part of maintaining *maat*, the divine order of the universe.

Egyptian houses reflected the home-based nature of women's work. The back of the house was always private. Here women could work and relax undisturbed by outsiders. Egyptian women were never confined to these rooms, however, except perhaps in cases of extreme wrongdoing. That is why a woman testifying before a law

Opposite: A woman of the Eighteenth Dynasty, portrayed in wood on her mummy case

This nineteenth-century painting brings to life a quiet moment in an Egyptian home. Many ancient paintings also show the Mistress of the House with a pet cat near or under her chair.

court would swear, "May I be sent to the back of the house if I am not telling the truth."

WORKING MOTHERS

The wife of a householder enjoyed the honored title Mistress of the House—and that is what she was. The house and everything that went on in it were her responsibility. Even though the husband was regarded as the head of the family, at home the wife was in charge—and it was an unhappy man who did not realize this. Scribes in training, therefore, were given this bit of advice to copy out:

> Do not control your wife in her house when you know she is efficient. Do not say to her "Where is it? Get it" when she has put something in its correct place. Let your eye observe in silence; then you will recognize her skill, and it will be a joy. . . . There are

many men who don't realize this, but if a man desists from strife at home he will not find it starting. Every man who establishes a household should hold back his hasty heart.

All women were expected to marry and have children—and with no reliable means of family planning, pregnancies were frequent. Caring for her children was the number-one responsibility of the Mistress of the House. Most of her other tasks were ones that could easily and safely be done in between seeing to the children's needs.

Food preparation took up a lot of a woman's time and energy. Since fresh-baked bread was the most important part of the Egyptian diet, she had to make sure that grain was ground almost every day. Making flour was exhausting work, which involved kneeling over a shallow stone trough and crushing the grain by rolling a roughly cylindrical stone over it repeatedly. Some women spent so much time at this job that their knees and toe bones were permanently deformed. It's no wonder that women who could afford to do so turned this work over to servants.

Most of the morning was spent preparing food, for the Egyptians ate their main meal at midday, when it made good sense to go inside and get out of the sun. The afternoon's major task was probably cloth making. In most households the women of the family produced all of the clothing worn by the family. Wealthy Egyptians had servants to do the bulk of this work. They might be supervised by a male or female overseer or by the Mistress of the House herself.

Nearly all Egyptian clothing was made of linen, a material that comes from the stems of flax plants. Growing, harvesting, and initial preparation of the raw flax was men's work; the women's work started with turning the flax fibers into thread. After cleaning the flax, the women sorted the long fibers and spliced the ends together

EAT LIKE AN EGYPTIAN

Bread was such an important food to the ancient Egyptians that by the New Kingdom, they had more than forty words for bread and cake of different kinds. The most popular types were baked in cone-shaped molds, formed by hand into semicircular loaves, or baked quickly on a flat stone—this last one turned out a little bit like modern pita bread. So for the first ingredient of your ancient Egyptian meal, try to get some whole-wheat pita.

Egypt was such a fertile country, thanks to the Nile, that cooks had an abundance of fresh ingredients to choose from. They didn't do much to dress up food—no fancy sauces and the like, although the addition of seasonings such as garlic, marjoram, dill, cumin, coriander, and cilantro was appreciated. The Egyptians don't seem to have served their food in separate courses: everything was laid out on the table (or on a mat on the floor) at once, and each person had a little bit of everything to eat.

Now that you have your bread and you know how to set up your meal, here are some foods that the ancient Egyptians commonly ate. Choose your favorites, and enjoy!

cucumbers	boiled beef
small raw onions	chicken roasted on skewers*
radishes	smoked or grilled fish
leeks	watermelon
chickpeas (often mashed with	dates
garlic and olive or sesame oil)	figs
lentils	grapes

*Chicken arrived in Egypt during the New Kingdom, but remained uncommon for some time. Most Egyptians were more likely to eat duck, goose, or other waterfowl than chicken.

Above: A woman servant kneels at a kneading trough to prepare a loaf of bread.

to make a rough yarn. Then, using a drop spindle, a woman spun this yarn into a tight, strong thread, which could be very fine. Two or three threads might then be spun together to make an even stronger fiber.

The next step was cutting the thread into suitable lengths and then setting up the weaving loom. Egyptian women typically wove on a horizontal loom that was pegged out on the floor. Some large houses had special weaving rooms, but the average woman probably set up her loom on the roof of her house. It almost never rains in Egypt, so she didn't have to worry about her work being ruined by the weather, and a screen of woven reeds or awning of palm fronds would protect her from the sun. Her children could play beside her as she worked, and she was probably glad to get up and play with them now and then, since kneeling over the loom for long stretches could become extremely tiresome.

This wooden model from a Middle Kingdom tomb shows two women weaving on horizontal floor looms.

For a very wide piece of cloth, two women often worked together, one squatting at each side of the loom. They passed the shuttle back and forth to each other, and no doubt enjoyed talking and telling stories as they wove. Eventually they would have a finished piece of linen cloth, which could be turned into clothing, sheets, or towels.

EARNING WAGES

A careful and industrious housewife could do quite a lot to increase her family's prosperity. If she wove extra cloth, baked extra bread, brewed extra beer, or grew extra vegetables in her garden, she could trade any of these items for other things that her family needed, or perhaps even for some little luxuries. Such exchanges were often informal arrangements between neighbors. Some women, however, took their surplus cloth or produce to market, where they would be paid in grain or other goods. We know a fisherman's wife was expected to clean her husband's catch and then take it to market. Other women no doubt assisted with their husbands' work in various ways, especially in the case of craftsmen who worked out of their homes.

Numerous women worked not in their own houses, but in other people's. Most often these workers were servants of various kinds. For example, a wealthy woman always employed one or more ladies' maids, and she might have nursemaids and wet nurses to help care for her children. Almost any fairly well-to-do family would hire at least one maid to help out with the household work.

As we have seen, another job sometimes held by women was that of weaving supervisor. There is evidence that some women worked as hairdressers and as makers of wigs, cosmetics, and perfumes, and that they also supervised other women workers in these fields. Two occupations held only by women dealt with the beginning and the end of life: midwife and professional mourner. Midwives assisted with

A musician plays a large harp to entertain banquet guests.

childbirth, while well-off families hired groups of mourners to participate in funerals—wailing, weeping, and making other displays of grief. Some ancient documents indicate that the mourners handled funeral arrangements as well.

Women also worked as entertainers and could earn good pay, status, and renown in this field. A wealthy family might employ its own troupe of musicians, singers, dancers, and acrobats to entertain at banquets, or a "freelance" troupe could be hired. Women worked as musicians and dancers at temples, too. The women played a variety of percussion instruments along with flute, harp, lute, and an ancient version of the oboe. Unfortunately, we don't know what the music sounded like, but we can guess that some of the songs with which women entertained banquet guests might have been similar to this one:

> Love, how I'd love to slip down to the pond,
> bathe with you close by on the bank.
> Just for you I'd wear my new Memphis swimsuit,
> made of sheer linen, fit for a queen—
> Come see how it looks in the water!
>
> Couldn't I coax you to wade in with me?
> Let the cool creep slowly around us?
> Then I'd dive deep down
> and come up for you dripping,
> Let you fill your eyes
> with the little red fish that I'd catch. . . .

FIVE

GROWING UP IN THE CITY

In ancient Egypt all babies were born at home. Usually one or two midwives helped the mother. But if something went wrong, there was little that could be done, and mothers and babies often died during or shortly after birth. As a New Kingdom saying went, "When death comes he steals the infant from the arms of the mother just as he takes him who has reached old age."

If all went well, however, after birth the midwife washed the baby, who was then returned to the mother's arms. The mother gave her baby a name right away. Often it was a family name—that of a grandparent, for example. It was generally considered a good idea to include the name of a god, if possible—many Egyptian names meant "Servant of" or "Gift of" a particular deity. Babies might also be named after members of the royal family or after beautiful things such as flowers. One ancient Egyptian name that is still popular is Susan, which meant "lotus."

Opposite:
A well-to-do woman nurses her newborn baby.

41

CAREFREE DAYS

Children were usually nursed for three years, although they probably started eating regular food some time before they were weaned. It appears that parents generally cared for their children very tenderly. Unlike in some other ancient cultures (such as those of the Greeks and Romans, who often abandoned unwanted babies), parents raised all the children born to them. Boys were favored slightly over girls, but girls seem to have received just as much parental affection.

Small children were constantly in the company of their mothers and other women of the family. Children could help the women with some tasks, but it seems that mainly they were free to play. Toys could be as simple as stray bits of flax, sticks and stones, or balls of claylike Nile mud. Children in wealthier families had

Some Egyptians had pet baboons, which were also sacred to the god of wisdom and writing, Thoth.

wooden or pottery dolls, doll cradles, puppets, tops, rattles, and toy animals. Some of the wooden animals were very cleverly made. Archaeologists have found mechanical toys worked by pulling a string: cats and crocodiles with mouths that opened and closed, a row of dwarves that danced on a little platform, and even a baker that kneaded dough. Children also liked to play a variety of games, including various ball games and something resembling leapfrog. Tomb paintings show boys wrestling and girls tossing small balls into the air, sometimes more than one at a time—it looks as though they are juggling!

Many Egyptians, young and old, were fond of animals. The most common pet was the cat, who also helped keep the house rodent-free. (The ancient Egyptian word for "cat," by the way, was *miw*.) Other favorite pets included dogs, geese, and monkeys.

Many Egyptians pampered their pets. This cat, sitting under a woman's chair, is enjoying its share of the fish served at a banquet.

BECOMING AN ADULT

We are not sure exactly when children began their serious education. Many kinds of skills and knowledge were learned at home, of course—and most children received all their education from their parents. It was expected that a boy would follow his father's occupation, and a girl her mother's. Girls were probably fairly young when they started practicing household skills, either in their own home or as servants in someone else's. Boys might be a bit older before they could really start learning their trade, depending on the amount of strength or skill it called for.

Occasionally the son of a craftsman was able to join the sons of scribes at school. Perhaps the following selection addressed such a boy:

> I have put you to school with the children of high officials, to teach and instruct you in this office which will lead to power and authority. See! I tell you the manner of the scribe in his (saying) "Prompt in your place! Write in front of your fellows. Put your hand to your clothes; see to your sandals." You bring your papyrus-roll daily with good intention. Don't be lazy! . . . Write with your hand; recite with your mouth; accept advice. . . . Enter into the ways of your teacher, and obey his instructions. Be a scribe!

From writings like this, it is clear that students learned by listening to lectures, copying from standard texts, and reciting other lessons from memory, and that they were also expected to uphold a certain standard of behavior and appearance. Teachers used a variety of techniques to motivate their pupils—including threats: "Do not pass the day lazily, or you will be beaten." The scribe Ani used

DID GIRLS LEARN TO READ?

There is good evidence that some princesses, at least, were taught to read and write—but what about ordinary girls? We know that they were not sent to school, but it is possible that some were privately taught by fathers, brothers, or even husbands with scribal training. The actions of some adult women indicate that they almost certainly had learned to read and write. For instance, in Deir el-Medina, the tomb workers' village, archaeologists found notes that seem to have been written by women. These were not formal documents, but brief notes to women friends and personal reminders—laundry lists, advice about dressmaking, and the like—not the sort of thing that a woman would have hired a scribe to write for her.

We also have a letter from a Theban scribe's wife, Hennutawy. She may have dictated it to a scribe, but the things she tells her absent husband make it seem likely that she'd had some education. Hennutawy's husband had asked her to take over his duty of supervising the unloading of two ships of grain while he was away. In her letter she informed him, "I went my own self and caused the grain to be received while I was there." She discovered, however, that the amount of grain was less than it should have been—someone had been stealing. "I checked out the *oipe*-measure and told them [the workers], . . . 'I shall find the grain wherever it is.'"

Still, Hennutawy and the women of Deir el-Medina would have been exceptional. Most girls had no need for a scribal education and no opportunity to pursue one. But the same was true of most boys, though to a lesser extent. Scribes made up a very small percentage of the population, and the majority of Egyptians, male and female, were illiterate.

Above: This container for scented ointment is in the shape of a servant girl carrying a jar. Like most Egyptians, such a servant would never have had the opportunity to learn to read.

Girls and young women often enjoyed acrobatics, which professional entertainers used in some of their dances.

what we might call guilt, reminding his son that he owed it to his mother to succeed in his studies because she had carried him through all the months of pregnancy, given birth to him, breastfed him, cleaned up his messes without complaint, and then "she put you to school when you were ready to be instructed in letters, while daily she waited for you with bread and beer in her house."*

In ancient Egypt, young people were considered to be adults in their early teens (which makes sense when we consider that most people could not expect to live much past age forty). Future scribes probably continued their education for some years more, but many others took up adult responsibilities almost immediately. This was especially true of girls, who were likely to be married very soon after puberty. Most boys were probably married by their late teens. The scribe Ani advised, "Take yourself a wife while you are young, so that she may give you a son. You should father him before you grow old and should live to see him become a man. Happy is he who fathers many children; he gains respect because of his progeny."

*Home-brewed beer was the common drink for most Egyptians. It was thick and sweet, less alcoholic and more nutritious than modern beers.

As far as we know, there was no formal wedding ceremony of any kind. The evidence suggests that a couple were considered married when they set up a household together (and were considered divorced if they stopped living together). It's likely that Egyptian marriages were often arranged by the parents. It also seems clear, though, that people frequently married because they had fallen in love. In any case, many love poems from the New Kingdom show that the Egyptians had a strong sense of romance, as in the following example:

The love of the beloved is on yonder bank;
The river lies between, and a crocodile lurks on
　　the sandbank.
But I go into the water, and I wade through the waves,
And my heart is strong in the flood.

The water is like land to my feet, the love of her
　　protects me.
It makes a water-magic for me!

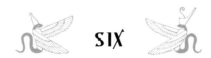

SIX

PASTIMES AND FESTIVITIES

What do they say every day in their hearts,
those who are far from Thebes?
They spend their day blinking at its name,
if only we had it, they say—
The bread there is tastier than cakes made with goose fat,
its water is sweeter than honey,
one drinks of it till one gets drunk.
Oh! that is how one lives at Thebes.

As this selection shows, the people of ancient Egypt's cities appreciated good living. Delights such as "cakes made with goose fat" were normally available only to the prosperous, of course, but even poor city dwellers had opportunities for relaxation and celebration.

There were many holidays throughout the year, when workers could rest from their labors. In some cases, too, people might be excused from their jobs for the day, and not just because of illness. We have examples from Deir el-Medina of men who stayed home

Opposite:
A funeral feast for an Old Kingdom princess—even in death, the Egyptians enjoyed a good banquet.

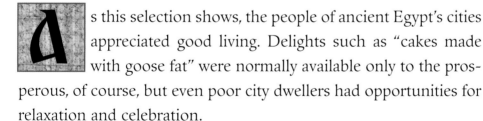

from work to build a new house, to weave—even to brew beer. The supervisors seem to have taken a relaxed attitude to this sort of thing; in any case, they always paid every worker his set monthly ration of grain. The tomb workers, of course, were highly esteemed for their special skills and enjoyed privileges not available to many other laborers. Still, with official days off, "excused absences," and holidays, some Egyptian workers, at least, could enjoy a great deal of free time. One surviving record from Deir el-Medina shows that during a fifty-day period, the entire crew of laborers had only eighteen working days!

FESTIVE GATHERINGS

All, or nearly all, Egyptian holidays were religious in nature. A highlight of these celebrations was a kind of parade that followed a set processional route from the temple of the goddess or god honored by the holiday. Priests carried the official statue of the deity in a litter or ceremonial boat. Other priests accompanied them with flowers and ostrich-feather fans. Musicians, singers, dancers, and offering bearers were also part of the procession, which was noisy and brilliant. The statue stopped at certain places along its route, allowing worshippers to approach it. Sometimes there might even have been a kind of play in which priests acted out a story associated with the deity.

Feasting would also have been part of the holiday merrymaking. A festival might be one of the few occasions when most Egyptians got to eat meat. Better still, there were some holidays when free food and beer were distributed by the government—and these might go on for days or even weeks!

Market stalls were sometimes set up during festivals, but even an ordinary market day could become a kind of miniature festival all its own. We don't know how often a town or neighborhood held mar-

Priests in procession
at a religious festival

ket days, but we know they occurred, thanks to tomb paintings that
show them in lively detail. Most of the traders were local people,
often women, displaying their extra cloth, vegetables, household
utensils, and other items on mats or in wide baskets. Both local and
traveling craftsmen offered their wares, too. Traveling barbers, who
often went street to street looking for customers, probably set up
stalls where they gave haircuts and shaves. There was nearly always
a stand selling beer—and in case anyone drank too much and got
out of hand, there was likely to be a security patrol, sometimes
assisted by trained monkeys.

Markets were often set up by the wharves where ships and boats
landed. A Nineteenth Dynasty scribe wrote, "The merchants sail
downstream and upstream, busy as bees, carrying goods from one
city to another, supplying him who has nothing." Many of these
"merchants" may actually have been government officials in charge

A scribe, his palette tucked under his arm and his document box behind him, unrolls a fresh sheet of papyrus so that he can make notes about a flock of geese for the pharaoh's tax records. Afterward, the goose herders may be able to take a few birds to market to trade for things they need.

of distributing goods from the pharaoh's storehouses. It seems, though, that merchants and sailors could trade on their own account, too. One tomb painting shows sailors leaving their newly docked ship to trade with women selling fish, vegetables, and bread.

Most of the shoppers at markets were men, and they had to bargain for what they wanted to buy. As mentioned earlier, the ancient Egyptians did not use money. The main form of payment for workers was a set ration of grain; "high-paying" jobs earned larger rations than "lower-paying" ones. Extra grain could be traded for other goods, which could then be traded for other goods, and so on.

An Old Kingdom tomb painting of a market has "captions" that give us some idea of how buying and selling were carried out. "Give me some of your product and I will give you sweet vegetables," says a vendor of onions and lettuce to a man with a jug of beer. At another stall, a woman encourages a shopper to trade her a fan for one of the pottery mugs she is offering: "See! Something you can drink from." And one satisfied shopper, exchanging a fish for a craftsman's work, exclaims, "I hand over for it the rest of what I have brought, with contented heart."

EVERYDAY AMUSEMENTS

The ancient Egyptians were often able to combine work and play, and not just by chatting and telling stories as they performed their daily tasks. Fishing, for example, was a popular activity. Many people of course made their livelihood from fishing, but for others it was a relaxing break from everyday cares—and if the outing was successful, there was the added bonus of a fish dinner. In one neighborhood of Memphis, archaeologists have found fishhooks made of a copper alloy and fishing weights made of limestone. The archaeologists also discovered plenty of fish bones, from at least twenty kinds of river fish.

A family outing in a Nile marsh. The father has just let fly his throwing stick to bring down a duck, and his little daughter tugs at his kilt to get his attention.

This humorous papyrus shows wolves herding a flock of goats while a lion and an antelope play the board game *senet*.

The Nile was home not just to fish, but also to numerous waterfowl. The bones of ducks, geese, and wading birds found in the same Memphis neighborhood show that people hunted waterfowl to put food on the table as well as for sport. Wall paintings show us that a day of hunting in the Nile marshes was often a family outing. The hunter went out in a small boat constructed from bundles of papyrus reeds. When he got to a likely spot, he stood up, balancing against the river current, and used a boomeranglike throwing stick to bring down birds in flight. Some paintings portray the family cat helping out by retrieving the birds, while the hunter's wife and children entertain themselves by picking lotus flowers.

Other active pursuits included ball games, wrestling matches, archery contests, and dart games (these involved throwing long darts at targets on the ground). Quieter games were enjoyed, too, especially board games. One was called serpent—perhaps it was a little like Snakes and Ladders?—and another was known as dog and jackal. The most popular board game of all was *senet,* which appears to have been a bit like parcheesi. Many *senet* boards have been found by archaeologists. The game's rules have long been a mystery, which Egyptologists have recently begun to solve.

From the tomb workers' village of Deir el-Medina comes evidence that some people liked to draw for fun. On flakes of stone or bits of broken pots, artists sometimes drew comic scenes that had nothing to do with decorating tomb walls or furnishings—for example, cartoonlike drawings that made fun of the boss. From Amarna comes an image of monkeys in a chariot, and at least one Egyptologist has noticed a resemblance between the monkey charioteer and the pharaoh Akhenaten. Probably the king would not have appreciated this—but his subjects clearly had a sense of humor. We can imagine them telling jokes and funny stories as they engaged in what was probably their favorite recreational activity of all: enjoying food and conversation with family and friends.

SEVEN

URBAN HARDSHIPS

An ancient Egyptian city could be a place of extreme contrasts, with the very rich and the very poor, the highly educated and the illiterate, living practically next door to one another. Wealth and education brought with them a variety of comforts, as well as privilege and power, while the poor had to contend with many more hardships. This can be seen not just in people's living conditions, but in such matters as the individual's relationship to the government and the justice system.

Law and order, for example, were very important to the ancient Egyptians, who tended to see the world in terms of order versus chaos. Certain aspects of law, however, seem to have been considered private matters. One of these was the protection of individuals and their property. The Medjay and other police forces were mainly concerned with guarding the interests of the state. For the most part, individuals had to take their personal protection into their

Opposite:
Under the direction of an overseer, a laborer carries jars of water slung from a pole across his shoulders.

57

SLAVE LABOR

A Libyan prisoner of war, portrayed in a bronze statuette. Prisoners of war often became slaves.

The least privileged people in an Egyptian city were slaves. Over the years there has been a great deal of uncertainty about slavery in ancient Egypt, which seems to have been rather different in nature from slavery in other ancient cultures. Some scholars have even concluded that there were no true slaves in Egypt. It is certainly hard to tell in most cases whether the servants we read about were slaves or free men and women.

We do know, without a doubt, that the New Kingdom was a period when Egyptian kings were conquering many neighboring areas. One result of the pharaohs' wars was the taking of numerous captives, especially women, who were brought back to Egypt and put to work. The foreign women were commonly sent to the weaving workshops that formed part of temple complexes. We also read about women who worked in bakehouses grinding flour, and we have to wonder if at least some of them might have been slaves. According to one papyrus, three women (out of a team of twenty-six) ground 7.25 sackfuls of flour (from 10.5 sackfuls of grain) in a single day. It seems more likely that this backbreaking work, at this pace, would have been done by slaves than by free women.

However hard their work, Egyptian slaves had various legal rights (which is why some scholars do not consider them slaves in the usual sense). Even though they themselves could be bought, sold, and rented out, slaves could buy, sell, own, rent, and inherit property. They could sometimes achieve a fairly high standard of living and could have servants or slaves of their own. Slave men could marry free women, and it appears that the children were regarded as free. To take just one instance, Thutmose III gave his barber a slave captured during a campaign in western Asia. The barber, in his will, provided for the future of the slave and his family: "He is not to be beaten, nor is he to be turned away from any door of the palace. I have given my sister's daughter . . . to him as wife. She shall have a share in [my] inheritance just like my wife and sister."

own hands. This was difficult for the poor, but naturally much easier for the wealthy, who could hire security guards for their homes. In addition, elite men were entitled to carry staffs as symbols of their rank or office—staffs that they could use as weapons if need be. Unfortunately, they sometimes used them to intimidate lower-ranking men, who could expect to be beaten for offenses large and small. It was rare for a poor man to challenge a rich one, in the law courts or anywhere else.

CROWDED CONDITIONS

Rich or poor, city dwellers were affected by urban crowding to a greater or lesser extent. Almost all towns grew without any kind of planning, and they could not expand into Egypt's valuable cropland. So new buildings were packed in against older buildings—and built on top of the ruins of still older ones. Sometimes the roofs of multistory houses nearly touched across the street. The crowding would have cut down on air circulation in many streets, which were mainly a confusion of narrow, twisting lanes. They were probably dark, too.

Privacy was almost unknown—although the ancient Egyptians most likely did not miss it, since it was something they weren't at all used to. Most of them would not have minded sharing the streets and even their houses with animals, either. Along with pets, many Egyptians kept food animals in their homes. For example, a family might catch a duck in the reeds along the Nile, then put it in a cage in the kitchen to fatten up until they were ready to eat it.

Getting rid of animal waste (and human waste, for that matter) was a problem, though. There were no garbage collection services. There may not even have been any kind of street cleaners to deal with manure from the donkeys that were the most common form of animal transportation in Egypt. People swept their houses often, but they discarded the sweepings into the street outside. When household waste and rubbish weren't tossed out into the street, they were taken to the nearest garbage dump. Some dumps were on the city outskirts; many, however, were right in the middle of things, and they could get pretty large. The garbage decayed rapidly because of the intense Egyptian heat, but it still attracted vermin. Because fresh building sites were scarce in most cities, every so often a dump would be burned or leveled so that it could be built over.

HEALTH HAZARDS

The crowding and minimal sanitation meant that Egyptian cities were not the healthiest places to live. Garbage dumps and grain stores were magnets for vermin that could, along with other problems they caused, carry diseases. Most people got their water from the Nile or canals; without a water-purification system of any kind, there was little or no protection from waterborne illnesses such as polio. The Egyptians did value personal cleanliness and washed frequently, and many shaved off their hair (women as well as men). These measures helped cut down on fleas and lice, but the average person was still exposed to many parasites and parasitic diseases. Egyptian medicine was fairly advanced, compared to some other ancient civilizations, but nevertheless there were numerous diseases and injuries that doctors could not treat. Usually, too, only prosperous people could even obtain the services of a doctor.

The steady north wind that filled the sails of ships southbound on the Nile could also be counted on to give city dwellers a break from the intense heat of the Egyptian sun. Unfortunately, this wind constantly blew sand into people's homes and workplaces—and even into their food. In addition, Egyptian bread contained tiny particles of stone, picked up during the process of grinding flour. Sand

In this tomb painting, a man crouches to drink from the Nile. Ironically, the water of the life-giving river was not always safe, and many people caught diseases from drinking and bathing in it.

and stone together ate away at people's teeth. Rich or poor, numerous Egyptians—especially if they lived into middle age—had all kinds of problems with their teeth and gums, from toothaches that were merely annoying to abscesses that could be fatal.

Although there were doctors who specialized in treating teeth, their medicines and medical techniques were limited. A New Kingdom document gives several techniques for dealing with various dental problems, such as: "To expel growth of purulency [infection] in the gums: sycamore fruit, beans, honey, malachite and yellow ochre are ground and applied to the tooth." For religious reasons, pulling a diseased tooth was not an option.

All city dwellers shared the same environmental hazards. People who did manual labor had added health risks. We have seen that a lifetime of grinding grain could deform a woman's knees and toe bones. The repetitive motions of many kinds of work led to aches and pains and, eventually, arthritis. Some jobs had other occupational hazards, as *The Satire on the Trades* never tires of pointing out. For example:

> The washerman washes on the shore
> With the crocodile as neighbor. . . .

Fishermen, too, had to worry about crocodile attacks. Hippos—very fierce when provoked—were another hazard for anyone whose work required them to be in or near the water.

The scribes praised their profession above all others, but even it had health hazards. A scribe sat nearly all day and might get little exercise, so he was liable to become overweight. The Egyptians regarded the rolls of fat typical of many older men in the scribal profession as signs of success and well-being, but we now know that those extra pounds could have had serious health consequences. And scribes themselves admitted that they were physically weaker than most other men. Even while trying to recommend his profession, one scribe wrote, "If you should take up a load and carry it, you would sink down, your feet trailing exceedingly, for you are miserably weak, all your limbs are wretched, and your body puny."

As we think about all the difficulties faced by urban Egyptians, we may wonder how they ever got through their days. Not only did they persevere through great challenges, but they managed to create works of art, buildings, and writings that still fill us with admiration. More than that, they managed to make friends, fall in love, raise families, take satisfaction in their work, and enjoy their leisure. These ancient people prove to us that hardships do not have to get in the way of either achievement or happiness.

GLOSSARY

adze a cutting tool used for shaping wood

alabaster a soft, translucent milky-white stone often carved into vases, cosmetic jars, and lamps

brazier a pan or other container for holding burning coals

dynasty a series of rulers who were usually related by family ties

hieroglyph a stylized picture that stood for a word, concept, group of consonants, or single consonant

inscription words written on or carved into lasting materials such as stone or metal

lapis lapis lazuli, a blue semiprecious stone much prized by wealthy Egyptians. It had to be imported through southwestern Asia from what is now Afghanistan.

necropolis a cemetery, or a group of connected cemeteries

obelisk a tall, four-sided column with a pyramid-shaped tip (like the Washington Monument in Washington, DC); obelisks were probably meant to symbolize the rays of the sun

papyrus a reedlike plant that once grew abundantly along the Nile; a writing material made from the fibers of this plant; a document written on this material. *Papyrus* is the source of our word *paper.*

pharaoh an ancient Egyptian king (or, occasionally, queen). The title *pharaoh*—or, in its original form, *per aa*—for an Egyptian ruler came into use during the New Kingdom. It initially meant "great house" and referred to the royal palace. (Compare this to the way we sometimes say "the White House" to mean the president.)

porter a laborer hired to carry burdens or to stand watch at a gate or door

relief a form of sculpture in which images are carved on a flat surface, either cut into it or projecting out from it

scribe a man who made his living by reading and writing. In a broader sense, the ancient Egyptians used *scribe* to mean an educated man, one who did not have to do manual labor but was qualified to serve in government or temple administration. A scribal education was so valued that even the highest nobles and officials proudly referred to themselves as scribes.

shuttle a tool used in weaving. The loom is set up with its warp, or long threads, already strung. The shuttle carries the thread for the weft, which goes crosswise over and under the warp.

stela a stone slab or plaque carved with words and/or images to commemorate an important person or event

villa a spacious house, often set within a large, walled compound; a mansion

FOR FURTHER READING

Berger, Melvin, and Gilda Berger. *Mummies of the Pharaohs: Exploring the Valley of the Kings.* Washington, DC: National Geographic, 2001.

Chrisp, Peter. *Ancient Egypt Revealed.* New York: Dorling Kindersley, 2002.

Douglas, Vincent, et al. *Illustrated Encyclopedia of Ancient Egypt.* New York: Peter Bedrick, 2001.

Green, Roger Lancelyn. *Tales of Ancient Egypt.* New York: Puffin Books, 1956 (reissued 2004).

Greenblatt, Miriam. *Hatshepsut and Ancient Egypt.* New York: Benchmark Books, 2000.

Harris, Nathaniel. *Everyday Life in Ancient Egypt.* New York: Franklin Watts, 1994.

Hart, George. *Ancient Egypt.* New York: Dorling Kindersley, 2000.

Hawass, Zahi. *Curse of the Pharaohs: My Adventures with Mummies.* Washington, DC: National Geographic, 2004.

Jovinelly, Joann, and Jason Netelkos. *The Crafts and Culture of the Ancient Egyptians.* New York: Rosen Publishing Group, 2002.

Manning, Ruth. *Ancient Egyptian Women.* Chicago: Heinemann Library, 2002.

Marston, Elsa. *The Ancient Egyptians.* New York: Benchmark Books, 1996.

Perl, Lila. *The Ancient Egyptians.* Danbury, CT: Franklin Watts, 2004.

Streissguth, Thomas. *Life in Ancient Egypt.* San Diego: Lucent Books, 2000.

Tames, Richard. *Ancient Egyptian Children.* Chicago: Heinemann Library, 2002.

ONLINE INFORMATION

Akhet Egyptology: The Horizon to the Past.
   http://www.akhet.co.uk/

The British Museum. *Ancient Egypt.*
   http://www.ancientegypt.co.uk/menu.html

Civilization.ca. *Mysteries of Egypt: Tutankhamun.*
   http://www.civilization.ca/civil/egypt/egtut01e.html

Fleury, Kevin. *Neferchichi's Tomb.*
   http://www.neferchichi.com/index.html

Kinnaer, Jacques. *The Ancient Egypt Site.*
   http://www.ancient-egypt.org/

Metropolitan Museum of Art. *The Art of Ancient Egypt: A Web Resource.*
   http://www.metmuseum.org/explore/newegypt/htm/a_index.htm

Museum of Fine Arts. *Explore Ancient Egypt.*
http://www.mfa.org/egypt/explore_ancient_egypt/
Nova Online. *Secrets of Lost Empires: Pharaoh's Obelisk.*
http://www.pbs.org/wgbh/nova/lostempires/obelisk/
Odyssey Online. *Egypt.*
http://www.carlos.emory.edu/ODYSSEY/EGYPT/homepg.html

BIBLIOGRAPHY

Aldred, Cyril. *The Egyptians.* 3rd ed. New York: Thames and Hudson, 1998.

Baines, John, and Jaromír Málek. *Ancient Egypt.* Cultural Atlas of the World. Alexandria, VA: Stonehenge Press, 1990.

Barber, Elizabeth Wayland. *Women's Work: The First 20,000 Years—Women, Cloth, and Society in Early Times.* New York: W. W. Norton, 1994.

David, Rosalie. *Handbook to Life in Ancient Egypt.* New York: Facts on File, 1998.

Editors of Time-Life Books. *Egypt: Land of the Pharaohs.* Alexandria, VA: Time-Life Books, 1992.

———. *Ramses II: Magnificence on the Nile.* Alexandria, VA: Time-Life Books, 1993.

Fagan, Brian. *Egypt of the Pharaohs.* Washington, DC: National Geographic, 2001.

Foster, John L., trans. *Ancient Egyptian Literature: An Anthology.* Austin: University of Texas Press, 2001.

James, Peter, and Nick Thorpe. *Ancient Inventions.* New York: Ballantine Books, 1994.

James, T. G. H. *Pharaoh's People: Scenes from Life in Imperial Egypt.* New York: Tauris Parke Paperbacks, 2003.

Mertz, Barbara. *Red Land, Black Land: The World of the Ancient Egyptians.* Rev. ed. New York: Dodd, Mead, 1978.

Romer, John. *Ancient Lives: Daily Life in Egypt of the Pharaohs.* New York: Henry Holt, 1984.

Shaw, Ian, ed. *The Oxford History of Ancient Egypt.* Oxford: Oxford University Press, 2000.

Silverman, David P., ed. *Ancient Egypt.* New York: Oxford University Press, 1997.

Trigger, B. G., et al. *Ancient Egypt: A Social History.* Cambridge: Cambridge University Press, 1983.

Tyldesley, Joyce. *Daughters of Isis: Women of Ancient Egypt.* New York: Penguin Books, 1995.

———. *Hatchepsut: The Female Pharaoh.* New York: Viking, 1996.

———. *Judgement of the Pharaoh: Crime and Punishment in Ancient Egypt.* London: Weidenfeld and Nicolson, 2000.

———. *Nefertiti: Egypt's Sun Queen.* New York: Viking, 1998.

———. *The Private Lives of the Pharaohs.* New York: TV Books, 2000.

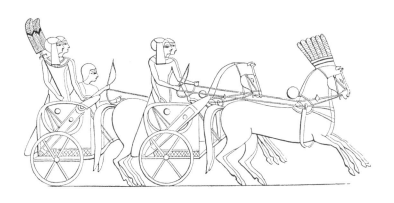

SOURCES FOR QUOTATIONS

This series of books tries to bring the ancient Egyptians to life by quoting their own words whenever possible. The quotations in this book are from the following sources:

Chapter 1: The Pharaoh's Cities

p. 5 "the pattern for every city": Fagan, *Egypt of the Pharaohs,* p. 186.

p. 5 "I did not leave": Tyldesley, *Hatchepsut,* p. 24.

p. 5 "all the wealth": ibid., p. 34.

p. 7 "Behold Akhetaten": Tyldesley, *Nefertiti,* p. 110.

p. 8 "His Majesty has built": Editors of Time-Life, *Ramses II*, p. 7.

p. 8 "beauteous of balconies": ibid., pp. 7–8.

Chapter 2: Public Places and Private Spaces

p. 14 "mountains, deserts": Tyldesley, *Nefertiti,* p. 113.

p. 21 "the sweet breath": translation provided by J. Brett McClain.

Chapter 3: Men at Work

p. 26 "This letter is sent": James, *Pharaoh's People,* p. 178.

p. 26 "is better than all": ibid., p. 142.

p. 26 "there is no profession": Mertz, *Red Land, Black Land,* p. 123.

p. 27 "A country-house": James, *Pharaoh's People,* p. 142.

p. 27 "A man is perished": Mertz, *Red Land, Black Land,* p. 122.

p. 28 "There is no tax": James, *Pharaoh's People,* p. 143.

p. 28 "any carpenter": ibid., p. 196.

p. 28 "at his work" and "stinks more": ibid., p. 181.

p. 28 "The potter": Silverman, *Ancient Egypt,* p. 99.

p. 29 "The jeweller": ibid., p. 99.

p. 30 "You chosen workmen": Editors of Time-Life, *Ramses II,* p. 56.

p. 30 "I am a craftsman": Mertz, *Red Land, Black Land,* p. 178.

Chapter 4: Mistress of the House

p. 34 "May I be sent": Tyldesley, *Daughters of Isis,* p. 86.

p. 34 "Do not control": ibid., p. 82.

p. 39 "Love, how I'd love": Foster, *Ancient Egyptian Literature,* p. 23.

Chapter 5: Growing Up in the City

p. 41 "When death comes": Tyldesley, *Daughters of Isis,* p. 79.

p. 44 "I have put you to school": James, *Pharaoh's People,* p. 140.

p. 44 "Do not pass": ibid., p. 141.

p. 45 "I went" and "I checked out": Editors of Time-Life, *Ramses II,* p. 108.

p. 46 "she put you": James, *Pharaoh's People,* p. 140.

p. 46 "Take yourself a wife": Tyldesley, *Judgement of the Pharaoh,* p. 92.

p. 47 "The love of the beloved": Mertz, *Red Land, Black Land,* p. 49.

Chapter 6: Pastimes and Festivities

p. 49 "What do they say": Romer, *Ancient Lives,* p. 4.

p. 51 "The merchants sail": James, *Pharaoh's People,* p. 248.

p. 52 "Give me some": Tyldesley, *Daughters of Isis,* p. 142.

p. 52 "See! Something you can": James, *Pharaoh's People,* p. 257.

p. 53 "I hand over": ibid., p. 257.

Chapter 7: Urban Hardships

p. 58 "He is not to be": Silverman, *Ancient Egypt,* p. 43.

p. 61 "To expel growth": Tyldesley, *The Private Lives of the Pharaohs,* p. 179.

p. 62 "The washerman": Barber, *Women's Work,* p. 198.

p. 62 "If you should take up": James, *Pharaoh's People,* p. 143.

INDEX

ABOUT THE AUTHOR

When Kathryn Hinds was in sixth grade, she wanted to be an Egyptologist more than anything. Eventually she discovered that her true calling was writing, but she still loves archaeology and ancient history. She has written a number of books for young people about premodern cultures, including the books in the series LIFE IN THE ROMAN EMPIRE, LIFE IN THE RENAISSANCE, and LIFE IN THE MIDDLE AGES. Kathryn lives in the north Georgia mountains with her husband, their son, and an assortment of cats and dogs. When she is not writing, she enjoys spending time with her family and friends, reading, dancing, playing music, gardening, knitting, and taking walks in the woods.

Fox Gradin, Celestial Studios Photography